Families Then and Now

Katie Peters

GRL Consultant Diane Craig,
Certified Literacy Specialist

Lerner Publications ◆ Minneapolis

Note from a GRL Consultant
This Pull Ahead leveled book has been carefully designed for beginning readers. A team of guided reading literacy experts has reviewed and leveled the book to ensure readers pull ahead and experience success.

Lerner Publications
An imprint of Lerner Publishing Group, Inc.
241 First Avenue North
Minneapolis, MN 55401 USA

For reading levels and more information, look up this title at www.lernerbooks.com.

Main body text set in Memphis Pro 24/39
Typeface provided by Linotype.

Photo Acknowledgments
The images in this book are used with the permission of: © Volodymyr Nikitenko/Shutterstock, p. 3; © chippix/Shutterstock, pp. 4–5, 16 (middle); © SeventyFour/Shutterstock, pp. 6–7, 16 (left); © Everett Collection/Shutterstock, pp. 8–9; © Yuganov Konstantin/Shutterstock, pp. 10–11, 16 (right); © Elzbieta Sekowska/Shutterstock, pp. 12–13; © Ladanifer/Shutterstock, pp. 14–15.

Front cover: © Rawpixel.com/Adobe Stock

Library of Congress Cataloging-in-Publication Data

Names: Peters, Katie author
Title: Families then and now / written by Katie Peters.
Description: Minneapolis : Lerner Publications, [2026] | Series: Let's look at families (pull ahead readers – nonfiction) | Includes index. | Audience: Ages 4–7 | Audience: Grades K–1 | Summary: "In the past, families listened to the radio. Now, most families watch TV. Accessible text and photographs help readers see what family time used to look like. Pairs with the fiction title, Just Like Nana"—Provided by publisher.
Identifiers: LCCN 2025011158 (print) | LCCN 2025011159 (ebook) | ISBN 9798765689882 library binding | ISBN 9798348028602 paperback | ISBN 9798765695180 epub
Subjects: LCSH: Families—Juvenile literature | Families—History—Juvenile literature
Classification: LCC HQ744 .P3935 2026 (print) | LCC HQ744 (ebook) | DDC 306.85—dc23/eng/20250716

LC record available at https://lccn.loc.gov/2025011158
LC ebook record available at https://lccn.loc.gov/2025011159

Manufactured in the United States of America
1 – CG – 12/15/25

Table of Contents

Families Then and Now

Families used to ride in wagons.

We ride in our car.

Families used to listen to radio shows.

We watch TV shows.

Families used to play together.

Today, families play together too!

Did You See It?

car seat

horse

popcorn

Index